Monarch Butterflies

by Helen Frost

Consulting Editor: Gail Saunders-Smith, Ph.D.

Consultant: Dr. Ronald L. Rutowski,
Professor of Biology, Arizona State University

Pebble Books

an imprint of Capstone Press
Mankato, Minnesota

Pebble Books are published by Capstone Press
818 North Willow Street, Mankato, Minnesota 56001
http://www.capstone-press.com

Library of Congress Cataloging-in-Publication Data
Frost, Helen, 1949–
 Monarch butterflies/by Helen Frost.
 p. cm.—(Butterflies)
 Includes bibliographical references and index.
 Summary: An introduction to the physical characteristics and behavior of
monarch butterflies.
 ISBN 0-7368-0229-0
 1. Monarch butterfly—Juvenile literature. [1. Monarch butterfly. 2. Butterflies.]
I. Title. II. Series: Frost, Helen, 1949– Butterflies.
QL561.D3F76 1999
595.78′9—dc21   98-31718
                                                                             CIP
                                                                             AC

Note to Parents and Teachers

The Butterflies series supports national science standards related to
the diversity and unity of life. This book describes the characteristics
and habits of monarch butterflies. The photographs support early
readers in understanding the text. The repetition of words and
phrases helps early readers learn new words. This book also
introduces early readers to subject-specific vocabulary words, which
are defined in the Words to Know section. Early readers may need
assistance to read some words and to use the Table of Contents,
Words to Know, Read More, Internet Sites, and Index/Word List
sections of the book.

2

Table of Contents

monarch egg

Monarch butterflies lay
eggs on milkweed plants.

6

Monarch caterpillars have stripes.

8

Monarch chrysalises are green with gold spots.

Monarch butterflies
are orange and black.

Monarch butterflies suck nectar from flowers.

migration of monarchs during autumn

Monarch butterflies migrate south during autumn.

They migrate to the same places every autumn.

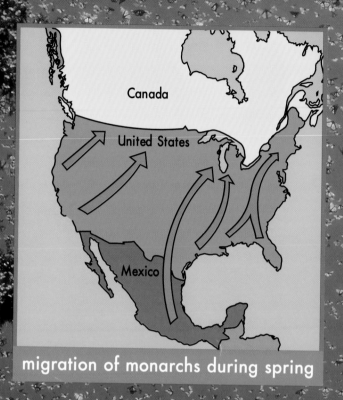

migration of monarchs during spring

18

They migrate north
during spring.

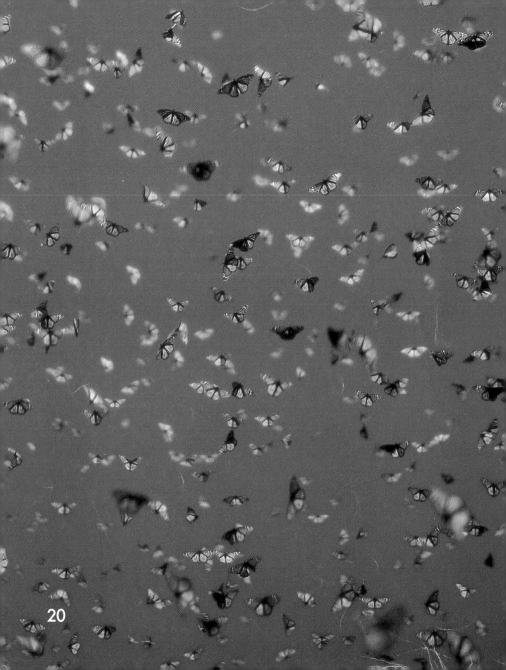

Monarch butterflies use
the wind to travel.

Words to Know

autumn—the season between summer and winter

chrysalis—the third life stage of a butterfly; caterpillars change into chrysalises; chrysalises change into adult butterflies.

migrate—to go away at a certain time of year to live in another place; millions of monarch butterflies migrate south during autumn and north during spring.

milkweed—a plant with milky juice and pointed pods; monarch butterflies lay eggs only on milkweed.

monarch—a large, orange-and-black butterfly; monarchs are common butterflies in North America.

nectar—a sweet liquid in flowers; monarch butterflies drink nectar.

Read More

Lasky, Kathryn. *Monarchs.* San Diego: Harcourt Brace, 1993.

Lavies, Bianca. *Monarch Butterflies: Mysterious Travelers.* New York: Dutton Children's Books, 1992.

Saunders-Smith, Gail. *Butterflies.* Animals: Life Cycles. Mankato, Minn.: Pebble Books, 1997.

Internet Sites

Children's Butterfly Site
http://www.mesc.nbs.gov/butterfly-faq.html

Danaus Plexippus: The Monarch
http://www3.pei.sympatico.ca/oehlkew/jplexipp.htm

Monarch Watch
http://www.MonarchWatch.org

Index/Word List

autumn, 15, 17
black, 11
caterpillars, 7
chrysalises, 9
eggs, 5
flowers, 13
gold, 9
green, 9
migrate, 15, 17, 19
milkweed, 5

nectar, 13
north, 19
orange, 11
plants, 5
south, 15
spots, 9
spring, 19
stripes, 7
suck, 13
wind, 21

Word Count: 56
Early-Intervention Level: 11

Editorial Credits
Colleen Sexton, editor; Steve Christensen, cover designer; Linda Clavel, illustrator;
    Kimberly Danger and Sheri Gosewisch, photo researchers

Photo Credits
Chuck Place, 12
Daybreak Imagery/Richard Day, 14
Fred Siskind, 10
KAC Productions/Kathy Adams Clark, 16, 20
Lior Rubin, 8, 18
Meggy Becker/David Clobes Stock Photography, 4
Robert McCaw, 1
Stuart Wilson, 6
Unicorn Stock Photos, cover